A TEACHER'S GUIDE TO UNDERSTANDING THE SACRAMENTS

SAMUEL M. POWELL

BEACON HILL PRESS
OF KANSAS CITY

Copyright 2011 by Samuel M. Powell and
Beacon Hill Press of Kansas City

ISBN 978-0-8341-2560-5

Printed in the
United States of America

Cover Design: Doug Bennett
Interior Design: Sharon Page

Unless otherwise indicated all Scripture quotations are from the *New Revised Standard Version* (NRSV) of the Bible, copyright 1989 by the Division of Christian Education of the National Council of the Churches of Christ in the USA. Used by permission. All rights reserved.

Library of Congress Cataloging-in-Publication Data

Powell, Samuel M.
A teacher's guide to understanding the sacraments / Samuel M. Powell.
p. cm.
Includes bibliographical references.
ISBN 978-0-8341-2560-5 (pbk.)
1. Sacraments—Study and teaching. 2. Baptism—Study and teaching. 3. Lord's Supper—Study and teaching. 4. Wesleyan Church—Doctrines. 5. Holiness churches—Doctrines. I. Title.
BV800.P69 2011
264'.07108—dc22

2010051631

10 9 8 7 6 5 4 3 2 1

CONTENTS

INTRODUCTION

The evangelical world seems confused about the sacraments. This does not mean individual evangelicals are confused; individuals usually have firm beliefs about the sacraments and why they are important. Rather, it's the evangelical world that displays a wide variety of conflicting opinions. Are sacraments necessary for salvation? Are they necessary for membership in a church? What do they signify? Why are they important? On these and other questions evangelicals can't seem to agree among themselves. The general confusion shows up in interesting ways.

On one Sunday a certain church happened to be performing baptisms. After all the candidates for baptism had been baptized, the pastor asked whether anyone else in the congregation wanted to be baptized. He indicated his willingness to baptize anyone who would profess faith in Jesus. This approach contrasts with the insistence of other churches that some period of instruction must precede baptism.

Or take the question of how important baptism is. The Southern Baptist Convention regards baptism as a necessary condition of church membership. It also limits participation in Communion to those who have been baptized.[1] However, Flood Church, a nondenominational church, views the matter differently. Flood regards baptism as a symbol that shows Jesus has entered a person's life and that the person has been spiritually transformed. Flood's statement of faith expressly denies that baptism is necessary to being a Christian, although it grants that baptism adds a certain richness to the Christian life and to the church.[2] For Baptists, membership and participation in the Lord's Supper require baptism; for Flood Church, baptism is a meaningful public statement but not otherwise important.

Or take this example concerning Communion. For the Assemblies of God, the Lord's Supper symbolizes the fact that Christians share in Christ's divine nature (referring to 2 Pet. 1:4). Communion, in other words, is *union* with and a participation in the Lord Jesus.[3] The Salvation Army, however, does not practice Communion (or baptism) and holds that God's grace is not linked to particular practices such as Communion.[4] Now both of these views cannot be correct. If the Lord's Supper expresses our sharing in Jesus' divine nature, then it does affect our salvation. If it doesn't affect our salvation, then it can't have much to do with sharing in Jesus' divinity.

There is also confusion about the practice of the sacraments. Most churches practice Communion as a celebration for the entire congregation. However, there are exceptions. Consider Calvary Chapel of Cheyenne, where the bread and cup of Communion are placed at the front of the sanctuary each Sunday. Members then decide on their own when they will partake of the elements. This puts a very individualistic spin on Communion. It is no longer an act of the community led by a pastor. Instead, individuals and families decide whether and when they will participate.[5] While this sort of do-it-yourself Communion is without doubt a great convenience to many, it does raise questions about the nature of Communion. Communion on demand for individuals seems out of step with the traditional congregational character of the Lord's Supper.

As a final example, an adult Sunday school class was discussing Paul's view of marriage. A member of the class stated, with great confidence, that marriage is a sacrament. Others around the table nodded their heads. The Sunday school teacher responded that for Protestants there are only two sacraments, baptism and the Lord's Supper. The teacher's words were received with shock and disbelief. The teacher took several minutes to explain that even though we call it *holy* matrimony, marriage is still not a sacrament for Protestants in the same way it is for Roman Catholics.

Evangelicals, who have in the past been very independent minded about many things, continue to think independently about the sacraments. Is this confusion a bad thing? Possibly it is, especially for Christians with a Wesleyan background. Here is why: The sacraments have an important place in churches with a Wesleyan heritage; however, these churches have been affected by the general confusion that we find in the evangelical world. As a result, such churches have become disconnected from their heritage and are unsure how to think about the sacraments.

How Did We Migrate to the State of Confusion?

Churches with a Wesleyan heritage trace their history back to John Wesley (1703-91) and the evangelical revival of the eighteenth century. Wesley was a priest in the Church of England. This means that Wesleyan churches are rooted in the soil of Anglican theology.

That Anglican heritage includes a strong appreciation for the sacraments. At the same time, other theological streams (Anabaptism, Pietism, and revivalism) feed into the Wesleyan tradition. The merging of the Anglican heritage with the other influences has brought about the state of confusion in which we find ourselves.

Anabaptism, Pietism, and revivalism have each made important contributions to Christianity. Each has been a significant voice calling for the revitalization of the church and contains truth that we need to hear today. However, every great movement, no matter how positive its effect, has unintended consequences. One of the unintended consequences of Anabaptism, Pietism, and revivalism was to reduce the importance of the sacraments. For some churches influenced by these movements, the sacraments have become quite trivial. For many others, the sacraments are still honored as a part of tradition but are practiced without much understanding, like someone who regularly has a car's oil changed as recommended by the owner's manual but does not really grasp why it's important.

Let's have a closer look at these three traditions.

Anabaptism began in Switzerland and Germany in the 1520s as the radical wing of the Protestant Reformation. It is represented today by groups such as the Mennonites, Amish, and Hutterites. Anabaptists have, in their long history, spoken with a clear voice on many significant issues, such as separation of church and state, the importance of nonviolence, and the church's need to distinguish itself from the surrounding society. However, in reaction to Roman Catholic theology they introduced serious changes to the theology of the sacraments.

First, the Anabaptists rejected infant baptism, insisting that baptism presupposes repentance, faith, and regeneration. Second, they described the Lord's Supper strictly in terms of remembrance. Centuries later, these ideas had the unintended effect of shifting the emphasis from what God does in the sacraments to what we do. Once the emphasis is put on what *we* do, baptism is seen as important because in it *we* declare *our* faith. And this is exactly how baptism is understood by many today. For example, a statement by the Southern Baptist Convention declares that (1) baptism is the believer's act of obedience; (2) that it symbolizes the believer's faith in Jesus, death to sin, and being raised to new life; (3) and that it testifies to the believer's faith in the general resurrection.[6] In this statement, all the emphasis falls on what believers do—their faith and testimony. There is no sense that baptism is God's act.

Similarly, an exclusive emphasis on remembrance in the Lord's Supper means that, once again, what is important is what believers do. For Southern Baptists, Communion, like baptism, is the believer's act of obedience. In Communion, believers are said to "memorialize" Jesus' death and to anticipate his return.[7] The Supper is for them *our* act of obedience and *our* act of memorializing.

Pietism arose in Germany during the late 1600s in an attempt to breathe life into Protestant churches. Like the Anabaptists, the Pietists made significant contributions to Christianity. They invented the idea of small-group Bible studies and insisted that Christianity is more about practice than about correct doctrine. But like Anabaptism, this movement produced some unintended consequences. For one thing, Pietism emphasized the "heart" over the "head" in religious matters. In the late 1600s, this was a welcome and helpful message; however, in later centuries this emphasis was exaggerated. To the extent that evangelicals today think of Christianity strictly as a matter of inward feeling and devotion, outward practices like the sacraments become comparatively unimportant. At best, they become ways of stimulating or expressing feeling. In such a pietistic environment, there is little support for sacramental practices.

Revivalism began in the 1800s during the camp meeting movement through the work of revivalists such as Charles Finney (1792–1875). This was, like Pietism, a powerful movement of renewal in the American Protestant churches. However, while revivals are important for the church, reviva*lism* so overemphasized dramatic conversion experiences that conversion came to be thought of as an experience. While experience is important in the Christian life, if we think of conversion exclusively as a dramatic, revivalistic experience, we cut conversion's connection to baptism—a connection the church had insisted on from its beginning. When we cut this connection, baptism becomes merely a testimony to our conversion, instead of being an instrument of conversion, as it has been understood since the beginning of the Christian church.

The unintended consequences of Anabaptism, Pietism, and revivalism are with us today whenever the emphasis falls on what we do in the sacraments (instead of what God does), whenever the sacraments are seen mainly as expressions of feeling, and whenever the only important thing in conversion is an experience. When these views are prevalent, the sacraments are either undervalued or practiced without much understanding.

1
WHAT IS A SACRAMENT?

A sacrament, to put it simply, is a practice instituted by Jesus Christ. However, we need a more thorough definition if we are to understand the sacraments. A classic definition of a sacrament was offered by Augustine of Hippo (354–430): a sacrament is a visible sign of God's grace.[8] Sacraments are visible because they are physical objects. But not every physical thing is a sacrament; sacraments are physical things that are signs. What, then, is a sign?

Some signs are arbitrary. Somebody, years ago, decided that stop signs should be a certain shape. In America stop signs have eight sides. But they would function just as well with a different shape or with fewer sides. The shape says nothing about the message of the sign. It's an entirely arbitrary shape. The only reason this particular shape signifies stopping is that in our society we've all agreed it should have that meaning. Similarly, think of the symbols we use in arithmetic (+, -, x, and so on). These symbols don't really bear any likeness to ideas such as addition and subtraction. We recognize them as symbols only because we've all agreed to use them for this purpose. If we wanted, we could come up with different symbols to express the same ideas. This is what it means to say that such symbols are arbitrary.

Other signs and symbols, however, are not arbitrary. An advertisement, for instance, signifies by showing us what's on sale—cars, fruit, or whatever. Here there is a likeness between the symbol (the photos in the ad) and what it symbolizes (the things on sale at the store). Or think about the phrase "free as a bird." Here we think of birds as symbolizing freedom because, unlike us, they can fly. Birds (for us) signify freedom because there is a likeness between their ability to fly wherever they want and our idea of freedom.

So, many signs and symbols are arbitrary; others bear a likeness to what they symbolize.

Sacraments are symbols of God's grace; however, they are not arbitrary symbols. They are likenesses. In what sense are they likenesses? Take baptism, for instance. Baptism, an act of physical washing, is a likeness of grace cleansing the soul. Communion, an act of physical eating, is a likeness of grace nourishing the soul. The physical aspect of each sacrament both symbolizes its spiritual effect and resembles that effect.

The fact that sacraments are signs (or symbols) creates a problem. In today's culture we often have a low regard for symbols. We may have the idea that symbols are less important than what they symbolize. We want the "real thing," not the symbol. As a result, we often undervalue the sacraments, regarding them as merely symbolic. But symbols are quite important. Few people would think a wedding ring unimportant because it's "only" a symbol. A wedding ring not only symbolizes the marriage but also confirms the marriage. Similarly, a gift may be only a token of love, but that doesn't make the gift unimportant or unneeded. On the contrary, it is through exchanging gifts that love is strengthened and confirmed. In the same way, sacraments symbolize the effects of grace but also strengthen and confirm those effects.

Sacraments, then, are visible signs or symbols of grace. It's important to emphasize that they are signs of *grace*. They symbolize and are likenesses of God's activity, presence, and revelation. That is why it is an utter disaster to define sacraments as an outward sign of an inward *experience*.[9] This way of thinking about sacraments gets everything wrong by putting the emphasis on us and on individualistic experience. The critical thing in the sacraments is not what we do or feel but what God does in the context of the church. In the sacraments God comes to us with grace and healing. A piece of art or music does not point to our experience; it points to the artist and what the artist is doing in and through the work. As with art, we do have to experientially receive the sacraments; however, as signs they point to what God is doing, just as the work of art points to what the artist is doing.

The sacraments, then, are acts of God. The church has insisted on this point ever since the fourth century during what is called the Donatist controversy.[10] One issue of the controversy was whether baptism is invalid if the priest administering the baptism is morally corrupt. Does the spiritual character of the priest affect the validity of the sacrament? Augustine expressed the view that even an unworthy priest can perform a valid baptism because baptism is actually God's act performed through the priest. The priest may be an unworthy instrument, but God is capable of using even unworthy instruments. The church adopted Augustine's view.

As signs of God's grace, the sacraments are closely connected to divine promises of salvation. They are, in a sense, God's way of enacting or performing the proclamation of salvation. Baptism is thus about the forgiveness of sin and the gift of the Holy Spirit (Acts 2:38). Communion then is about sharing in Christ's body and blood (1 Cor. 10:16). The connection to divine promises tells us why, as Martin Luther (1483–1546) insisted, sacraments should always be accompanied by Scripture. In fact, it's best to see sacraments and Scripture as simply two ways in which God's promises are declared to us. In Scripture we receive them verbally; in the sacraments we receive them in visible signs.

2

WHY ARE THE SACRAMENTS IMPORTANT?

Sacraments are important for several reasons. For one thing, there is the *testimony of the New Testament*. The New Testament contains clear commands to be baptized and to celebrate Communion. In Acts, Peter tells the crowd to repent and be baptized for the forgiveness of sin (2:38). In Matthew's gospel Jesus commands the apostles to make disciples by baptizing and teaching (28:19-20). In John's gospel Jesus says that no one can enter the kingdom without being "born of water and Spirit"—a clear allusion to baptism (3:5). At the Last Supper, Jesus told his disciples to "take, eat" (Matt. 26:26) and to do it "in remembrance" of him (Luke 22:19). There can be little question that New Testament writers expected Christians to be baptized and to participate in the Lord's Supper.

The importance of the sacraments also rests on the *authority of Christian tradition*. Christian writings immediately after the age of the apostles show us that baptism and the Lord's Supper were practiced universally and faithfully. All through the early centuries of Christianity, through the Middle Ages, and through the Reformation era, baptism and the Lord's Supper were practices of critical importance.

Theological considerations provide a third reason for the importance of the sacraments. The sacraments relate to the idea of revelation and the doctrine of creation. Revelation is about God's self-disclosure—God's acts of speaking to us and becoming present among us. How does revelation happen? Does it always come to us in a verbal form (as in the Bible and preaching)? Or can revelation come to us through physical things as well? The Bible itself indicates that things in the created world can indeed be revelatory. Psalm 104 testifies to the many ways the world exhibits God's wisdom. Romans 1:20 tells us that created things show forth God's power and nature. The biblical idea of revelation, then, contains a powerful affirmation of the physical world. The Christian idea of a sacrament is simply this idea of revelation in creation joined to the idea of grace. *The sacraments are the revelation of God's grace through physical means.*

The doctrine of creation is thus important for the idea of the sacraments. The doctrine of creation tells us that, in spite of sin, the world remains the object of God's love and that the world is not alien to God. This is a vital point, because we are sometimes tempted to think that the world is so fallen that it is no longer a place where God may dwell. In the second and third centuries, this view was held by Christians called Gnostics. For them, the created world was hopelessly involved in fallenness; in no way could it be a home for God. Against this view the church insisted that this world is still God's creation and that God is at home in this world. The doctrine of creation thus supports the idea of the sacraments by showing that *God dwells in the world of physical things such as sacramental bread and water.* God comes to us in and through the things that God has created. Sacramental elements such as bread and water are special ways in which God comes to us, because (in the context of worship) they are consecrated for that purpose.

The doctrine says something else. It reminds us that we are creatures of flesh and blood. This means that we receive God's revelation as bodily creatures and through the body. We acquire scientific and everyday knowledge through bodily means such as seeing and hearing. We also receive grace through bodily means such as reading Scripture, hearing preaching, and receiving the sacraments. The doctrine of creation tells us that the physical elements of the sacraments are important because we, as part of the created world, are physical beings whose souls are nourished through bodily means. It has to be this way because we are not pure, disembodied spirits. Whatever comes to be in our spirits must come through our bodies.

These beliefs about revelation and creation come together in the doctrine of the incarnation—the belief that Jesus Christ is the union of God and humanity. Christianity stands or falls with the belief that God came into the world as a flesh-and-blood human being. The supreme revelation of God was a physical being, Jesus Christ. In the incarnation, creation participates with God in the act of revelation; here God and the created world are joined together in a personal union. The idea of the sacraments is in some ways just an extension of the idea of incarnation. In both cases, God's grace and revelation approach us in and through something in the created world. So Christianity is a sacramental religion because it is the religion of the incarnation.

3

DISAGREEMENTS ABOUT THE SACRAMENTS

The Donatist controversy was mentioned earlier; however, this was not the church's only disagreement about sacramental theology and practice.

How Many Sacraments?

One question that is still with us today is about the number of sacraments. Protestants affirm two sacraments, baptism and Communion. The Orthodox churches have never established a precise number of sacraments, but instead have a number of sacramental practices besides baptism and Communion. In the 1500s the Roman Catholics fixed the number of sacraments at seven (baptism, confirmation, Communion, ordination, marriage, penance [today called reconciliation], and anointing the sick). Some churches (such as Quakers and the Salvation Army) do not have sacraments. A few (such as the Church of God in Christ) rank foot washing as an "ordinance" alongside baptism and Communion.

Why the disagreement? For Protestants, sacraments are those practices Jesus explicitly commanded as a formal practice of the church. For Catholic and

Orthodox Christians, a sacrament is a church practice that the Bible commands or endorses. Catholics, for example, regard marriage as a sacrament because, even though Jesus did not explicitly command marriage, God blesses marriage. For Protestants, however, it is not a sacrament because Jesus did not command it as a formal practice of the church.

Sacrament or Ordinance?

Another question concerns the word "sacrament." This word makes some Protestant Christians nervous, and they prefer the word "ordinance." To them, "sacrament" has too many Catholic associations. "Ordinance," for them, emphasizes Jesus' act of ordaining these practices. However, the Anglican heritage of Wesleyans teaches them not to be frightened of the term "sacrament." It's a traditional term and has been used for centuries. It's important that Jesus ordained these sacraments, but there is no need to invent a new term to emphasize that fact. As a result, Wesleyan churches refer to these practices as sacraments in their articles of faith.

Who Can Perform a Sacrament?

Finally, questions have arisen about who can perform sacraments. As observed earlier, sacraments are acts of God. Nonetheless, the church has thought about the human instruments that God uses and has taught that, as a rule, only ordained clergy should perform sacraments. This rule rests on the belief that God has invested the church with authority, as when, in Matt. 16:19, Jesus gave to Peter the keys of the kingdom, with the power of binding and loosing. The church has generally understood this to mean that Jesus gave to the apostles authority to govern the church. They in turn ordained bishops and pastors to oversee the church. Bishops and pastors, then, have the primary responsibility for the church's well-being and ministries. Under their supervision, sacraments are performed and taught in a proper and authentic way. Of course, the church always recognized (especially for baptism) emergency situations, when administration of the sacraments was critical. In these rare situations, the church has authorized laypeople to perform sacraments; however, these exceptions to the rule are just that—exceptions. As a general practice, the church has insisted that because of the importance of the sacraments for the church's integrity and well-being, they may be performed only by ordained clergy.

4
UNDERSTANDING THE SACRAMENTS

The New Testament, especially John's gospel, supplies much material for reflecting on the sacraments. Think about the way this gospel uses the symbols of light (1:4-5, 9 and chap. 9), water (4:7-15), and bread (6:32-35). In each of these passages, something physical and everyday becomes a vehicle of divine revelation and grace. Jesus is the Light of the World, who, in chapter 9, brings both physical and spiritual sight to a blind man. Jesus brings the water of life to the Samaritan woman, who comes to the well to draw physical water. Jesus is the bread from heaven, who provides not only physical bread (in the feeding of the five thousand) but also spiritual bread, which is his flesh. In each of these symbols, there is a likeness between the physical thing and the effect of God's grace: the light Jesus brings to the blind man's eyes signals the light from heaven. The well water the woman wants symbolizes the water of eternal life. The bread that feeds the crowd symbolizes the bread from heaven. John's gospel is thus an intensely sacramental gospel. In it worldly, everyday realities become tools of God's revelation and grace.

With this rich vein of sacramental theology in John's gospel, we can spell out a few aspects of the sacraments.

The Sacraments as Media

If the Bible is clear about anything, it's that God cannot be seen (John 1:11; 1 Tim. 6:16). But it's also clear that we come to know God through physical things. The prophets give us numerous examples: Jeremiah heard God speaking while observing a potter at work (Jer. 18:1-12). Ezekiel "saw" God as he experienced a storm (Ezek. 1). Amos received the word of God while beholding a basket of fruit (Amos 8:1-3). In each case, God came to the prophet in and through some physical reality. The sacraments are simply this principle established in a practice of the church. They are the customary physical realities by which we know the God who cannot be seen.

The Sacraments as Mirrors

A mirror is an interesting thing. We look at a mirror and see something else—whatever the mirror is reflecting. We see things *in* the mirror as we look *at* the mirror. It is in this sense that sacraments are mirrors: we see the bread and the cup of Communion, but in them we see the grace of God. We see the water of baptism, but as in a mirror, we see God at work, forgiving and imparting the Holy Spirit.

The Sacraments as Tokens

A token is a kind of symbol: "This ring I give you as a token of my love . . ."[11] We often think of gifts as tokens. We have, in America, a proverb that it's not the gift but the thought that counts. This proverb is typically expressed whenever someone is unable to give a gift that would otherwise be expected. But we all know that in the normal course of life, thoughts alone do not substitute for tokens; this is why we rather insist on the giving of rings in a wedding ceremony—tokens are important. It is also why the giving of actual gifts in friendship and marriage is vital. Assertions of love without tokens of love become empty words. The truth is, we need physical tokens to assure us of love and goodwill. The sacraments are, in this sense, tokens of the greatest importance. They proclaim God's love and grace to us more powerfully than would words alone.

The Sacraments as Performance

Music helps us understand the idea of sacraments. Music on the printed page is, in a sense, not really music. To be fully music, it must be performed for an audience. It is performance that actualizes notes on a page and turns them into actual music. Think, then, of the sacraments as the performance of grace. God is the performer; we are the instruments as well as the audience. Without the performance of sacraments and sacramental practices, the idea of grace remains abstract. With performance grace is actualized and made concrete in the soul.

BAPTISM

5
THE HISTORY OF BAPTISM

Where and when did baptism begin? Baptism was not, so far as we know, practiced by Jews in the time of Jesus. However, Jews did practice something similar, ritual bathing. Archeology has discovered pools apparently used for ritual washing, and John's gospel mentions jars of water used for purification (2:6). It seems that many Jews, especially priests, were concerned to purify themselves with water, especially in preparation for worship.

The first incidence of baptism is that of John the Baptist. For John, baptism was an act of repentance in preparation for the Messiah and God's kingdom. His preaching was aimed primarily at Jews, whom John saw as ill-prepared for the coming judgment. Baptism was the symbolic event by which Jews would prepare for the end times and for judgment.

The early church adopted John's practice of baptism; however, in a Christian context the meaning changed considerably. For Paul, baptism was dying and rising with Jesus (Rom. 6:3-4). In Acts it is connected with receiving the Holy Spirit (2:38). It is also understood as cleansing (22:16; see also 1 Cor. 6:11; and Titus 3:5).

By around AD 200, the practice of baptism had become fairly well defined. Having moved from a mainly Jewish context to a mainly Gentile context, the church found it necessary to preface baptism with a lengthy period of instruction (catechesis). With increasing numbers of Gentile converts, the church could not presuppose that the knowledge or morality of baptismal candidates was appropriate for church membership. The church thus established processes for instructing candidates in Christian doctrine. At the same time, the church insisted that candidates reform their lives and tried to ensure that by the time candidates were baptized, they had forsaken sin and were living appropriately.

At some point Christians began having their infants baptized. We don't know where, when, or why this practice began. It is possible that infants were baptized in the New Testament period; we read several times in the New Testament that entire households (i.e., extended families) were baptized (Acts 16:34; 1 Cor. 1:16). These households may have included infants. All we really know is that by the early 200s Christian writers mentioned that this practice was taking place. Within a few centuries infant baptism had become common.

The details of the baptismal ceremony for adults were also well established by the second century. The church typically conducted baptisms at Easter. Prior to the ceremony, candidates would fast; this exhibited their repentance and transition from their former life in the Gentile world. Priests would offer prayers of exorcism to eliminate from the candidates all final traces of the demonic. Then candidates would be anointed with oil, and the bishop would lay hands on them. The oil and laying on of hands signified the reception of the Holy Spirit. Candidates would next make a public profession of faith by reciting something comparable to the Apostles' Creed. Following the baptism, the new Christians were given new clothing, symbolizing their new life in Christ, and they then participated for the first time in Communion.

The church of the first few centuries also elaborated a rich theological understanding of baptism. For one thing, the church saw baptism as an initiation into the holy people of God. They likened the church to Noah's ark (salvation inside; destruction outside) and saw baptism as the moment when one becomes a part of the church. The church thus saw baptism as necessary for salvation. Except for those who died as martyrs or in the process of catechesis, no one, they held, could be saved without baptism. This was because baptism marked the moment when a person's sins were forgiven and he or she received the Holy Spirit (Acts 3:28). Because of its connection with receiving the Spirit, baptism was also understood as the moment when a person was born again (in regeneration) and was initially made holy (sanctification).

An important development came with the doctrine of original sin. According to this doctrine, human beings inherited from Adam a fallen nature and guilt. With the development of this doctrine, infant baptism received a new and important support; although infants did not need baptism for forgiveness of their own sins (since they hadn't yet committed any), they needed it for forgiveness of the guilt of original sin.

In summary, the early church saw in baptism an event of the greatest significance. It was the turning point in a person's spiritual life.

Clearly baptism is not the beginning of God's work within us. Long before we are baptized, God's grace has been leading us to repentance and faith. Nonetheless, baptism is the event in which the effects of grace are realized in divine acts of rebirth, adoption, and forgiveness.

As far as the theology of baptism goes, little changed until the 1520s. This decade saw the rise of the Anabaptist movement, which insisted that infant baptism was not valid. For them, only "believer's" baptism (i.e., adult baptism) was valid, because valid baptism required repentance and faith. Most Protestant churches, however, including the Anglican tradition, continued to affirm the validity of infant baptism.

6
THE THEOLOGY OF BAPTISM

What does the church believe about baptism? Let's start with the question, "What constitutes a valid baptism?" This question arises when the church has to think about receiving into membership someone who was baptized by a heretical group. Is a baptism performed by heretics valid or not? You might think that the church would just routinely rebaptize heretics, but the church has historically had a strong bias against rebaptism. It thus became important to establish criteria for a valid baptism.

There are three things required for a valid baptism. First, it has to involve water; second, it must be accompanied by a proclamation of God's Word; third, it must be performed in the name of the Father, Son, and Spirit. There's not much controversy about the first and second points. The third point has been the critical one. The church initially experimented with rebaptizing heretics who joined the church; however, by AD 400 the church decided that baptism by heretics, if performed in the name of the Trinity, is valid and does not require rebaptism.

Beyond these necessary requirements, there are a couple of very important practices. We've already mentioned one—sacraments such as baptism will normally be performed by ordained clergy. The other highly important practice has to do with the consecration of the water. This is an ancient practice in which the church prays that the Spirit will consecrate the water so that those baptized can truly be "born of water and Spirit" (John 3:5).

What does baptism signify? As the point of transition into the holy people of God and into salvation, baptism has a rich variety of meanings. We've already touched on some of these meanings, but now we will examine them, along with several others, in greater detail.

Forgiveness

Baptism signals the forgiveness of sins. The key passage here is Acts 2:38: "Repent, and be baptized every one of you in the name of Jesus Christ so that your sins may be forgiven; and you will receive the gift of the Holy Spirit." But why is baptism a sign of forgiveness? This leads to another meaning of baptism, cleansing.

Cleansing

Several New Testament passages portray baptism as an act of washing or cleaning. Acts 22:16, for instance, commands us to "be baptized, and have your sins washed away." Hebrews 10:22 urges, "Let us approach [God] with a true heart in full assurance of faith, with our hearts sprinkled clean from an evil conscience and our bodies washed with pure water." In both passages, baptism effects a cleansing—sin is washed away, hearts are sprinkled clean.[12]

This aspect of baptism is powerfully symbolized in the movie *The Shawshank Redemption*. Toward the end of the movie, Andy Dufresne, wrongfully convicted and imprisoned, breaks out of prison by crawling through a sewer pipe. Emerging from the end of the pipe, Andy falls into a river or lake and begins stripping off his clothes soaked with filth. Stripped of those clothes and cleaned by the fresh water, he makes his escape to freedom, clothed with clean clothes stored in a bag. In this scene we get an image of baptism—the water that cleanses and thus brings us to a new life.

Receiving the Holy Spirit

Because baptism is a cleansing, it marks the transition from sin to salvation. Entry into salvation means we forsake the spirit of the world and receive the Spirit of God. Clearly we should not think that the gift of the Spirit is mechanically tied to baptism. In Acts 10 Cornelius receives the Spirit before being baptized (vv. 44-48), while in Acts 8, although Philip baptizes the Samaritans, they do not receive the Spirit until Peter and John lay hands on them (vv. 15-17). Nonetheless, Acts 2:38 clearly associates baptism with receiving the Spirit, and the church has always emphasized this point.

Putting on Christ

For Paul, baptism is a transition from the old to the new. He compared it to the Roman ceremony in which young boys put on, for the first time, an adult robe (or toga). Putting on the adult toga signified, in Roman society, that the boy had become an adult. Thinking of this ceremony, Paul stated that "as many of you as were baptized into Christ have clothed yourselves with Christ" (Gal. 3:27). Baptism thus signifies that we are no longer spiritual minors who are no better than slaves (4:1) and that we have instead clothed ourselves with Jesus Christ and entered into spiritual adulthood.

Dying and Rising

For Paul, the most important thing about the Christian life is our identification with Jesus' suffering, death, and resurrection. To be a Christian is to share in Christ's sufferings and his death, so that we can share in his resurrection (Phil. 3:10-11). Baptism thus is a sign of our sharing in Christ. "All of us who have been baptized into Christ Jesus have been baptized into his death. . . . We have been buried with him by baptism into death, so that, just as Christ was raised from the dead by the glory of the Father, so we too might walk in newness of life" (Rom. 6:3-4; see also Col. 2:12). Because baptism is an event in which we die and are raised in Christ, the New Testament connects baptism with rebirth, as when Titus 3:5 speaks about the "water [literally, washing] of rebirth and renewal by the Holy Spirit" and when Jesus speaks of "being born of water and Spirit" (John 3:5).

Union with Christ

Because in baptism we share in Christ's death and resurrection, Paul understood baptism as an event in which we are united with Christ: "For in one Spirit we were all baptized into one body . . . and we were all made to drink of one Spirit" (1 Cor. 12:13). Baptism is thus an act of incorporation. In it we become part of Christ's body and thus come to share in his Spirit.

7

DISAGREEMENTS ABOUT BAPTISM

The practice of baptism has raised many questions and prompted much discussion among Christians for centuries. Several of these issues are still debated today. Let's examine some of the more significant ones.

Salvation Without Baptism?

One question that often arises is whether we can be saved without baptism. The answer to this question requires us to recognize that although all things are possible with God, the New Testament contains standards of practice for the church. In other words, there is a difference between what is permitted and what is normative. Because all things are possible with God, people such as the repentant thief on the cross (Luke 23:39-43) can be saved without baptism. At the same time, the church should not allow exceptions such as this to overthrow the normative practice of baptism that Jesus commanded. The early church quickly perceived that some people undergoing catechesis die before being baptized. In these cases, the church understood that the desire for baptism and intention to be baptized is sufficient. So the church has never insisted on the absolute necessity of baptism. However, the church should not have to tolerate believers who simply refuse to be baptized.

Immersion or Pouring?

Another issue that has been debated concerns the mode of baptism, that is, whether there is only one authentic way of baptizing. Traditionally, the church favored full immersion in water but did not think of immersion as the only valid mode. In some contexts, pouring water onto the baptismal candidate became the custom. This issue became controversial in the 1500s, when Anabaptists in Poland began to insist that immersion is the only valid mode of baptism. In the 1600s, some English Baptist groups adopted this view. In America, the Restoration Movement (now embodied in the Churches of Christ and Disciples of Christ) likewise insisted on immersion as the only valid form of baptism. The issue boils down to this: does the New Testament prescribe a single and particular mode of baptism? If so, then the church is obliged to employ that mode. If not, then the church is free to use any mode that is practical. The churches in the Wesleyan tradition have long held that the New Testament does not prescribe a particular mode of baptism. As a result, they regard both immersion and pouring as acceptable forms of baptism.

Infant Baptism?

Perhaps the longest running debate about baptism concerns infant baptism. As observed earlier, beginning in the 1520s Anabaptists rejected the practice of infant baptism and held that only adult baptism is valid. Since, from New Testament times onward, baptism had been linked with the forgiveness of sin (including original sin), Anabaptists had to think about why infants and children did not need baptism for forgiveness of the guilt of original sin. The Anabaptists' response was to argue that children are not held accountable for sin until they reach the age of moral responsibility and reason. Until then they exist in a state of innocence.

The Anabaptist rejection of infant baptism caused other Protestants to consider this practice carefully. Martin Luther in particular devoted a lot of attention to this question. Luther strongly supported infant baptism and developed several arguments for it. For one thing, he believed that infants can be baptized because they can have faith, just as John the Baptist seemed spiritually responsive while still in utero (Luke 1:41). This view contrasted with that of the Anabaptists, who believed that only adults can have faith. Luther also felt that because the kingdom belongs to children (Mark 10:14), they should be baptized. He also argued that infants and children were probably included in the whole households that were baptized in New Testament times. Luther additionally argued that baptism is the New Testament equivalent to circumcision in the Old Testament, both signifying membership in the holy people of God. If baptism is truly equivalent to circumcision, then infant baptism is mandated. Finally, he argued that since the Bible does not prohibit infant baptism, the tradition and custom of the church should remain in effect.

John Calvin (1509-64) also responded to the Anabaptist challenge. Like Luther, he felt that the new covenant, like the old covenant, is accompanied by signs. In the old covenant, the sign of belonging to the people of God was circumcision. In the new covenant, however, there is a different and better sign, baptism. Since infants were circumcised in the old covenant, they should be baptized in the new covenant.

Doctrinally speaking, little has changed on this issue in the last few centuries. Catholics, Orthodox, Anglicans, Presbyterians, Lutherans, and Methodists still baptize infants. Anabaptists do not. What has changed is the rise of movements inspired by Anabaptist theology. These movements include the various Baptist traditions, Restorationist churches (Church of Christ, Disciples of Christ), and the multitude of nondenominational congregations. The growth of these movements means that, especially in America, the evangelical tradition has come to have a bias against infant baptism.

Where do churches with a Wesleyan background stand on this issue? Some (such as the Church of God, Anderson) do not practice infant baptism. Many (such as the Church of the Nazarene, the Free Methodist Church, and the Wesleyan Church) do; however, even in these churches infant baptism is not common. What has happened is that the Anglican heritage of Wesleyan churches has been mixed with the influence of Anabaptist and Restorationist theology. The result is a bit of confusion, with some churches practicing infant baptism while others do not and with some churches that accept infant baptism not practicing it much. A sign of this confusion is that many Wesleyan churches make provision for both infant baptism and infant dedication. They have, in essence, decided to allow their members to choose which ritual to use. Those whose theology fits in with John Wesley's Anglican heritage may choose infant baptism. Those who are more comfortable with the Anabaptist and Restorationist tradition will probably choose infant dedication.

So, is there any difference between infant baptism and dedication? Although the two rituals appear similar, there is really a considerable difference. Infant baptism is a sacramental sign. It signifies the presence of grace in the infant and declares that the infant belongs to the people of God. Above all, it signifies what God has done and is doing. It is, in other words, a powerful instance of God's prevenient grace, which works in us before we are aware or can respond. The ritual of infant dedication, however, focuses on the infant's parents. The Church of the Nazarene's ritual illustrates this fact when it states that "in presenting this child for dedication you signify not only your faith in the Christian religion but also your desire that he (she) may early know and follow the will of God, may live and die a Christian, and come unto everlasting blessedness."[13] We see here that infant dedication is really about the parents' faith and desires. It is a way of encouraging parents to be faithful in raising their children.

Wesleyan churches that affirm infant baptism should perhaps practice it more diligently and be more intentional about teaching and preaching about it. In turn, they should also be more attentive to postbaptismal education (catechesis). An important step to making these changes would be recognizing that infant baptism and infant dedication serve two distinct purposes: baptism proclaims what God is doing; dedication is a ceremony in which parents affirm their intention to raise their children in a godly way.

Instruction Before Baptism?

As mentioned earlier, at the end of one church service, the pastor invited anyone who wished to be baptized to come forward, where they would be immediately baptized. The pastor made it very clear that the only requirement for baptism is faith in Jesus. No other instruction in the Christian faith was deemed necessary.

This approach to baptism makes sense if baptism is a declaration of our faith; once someone has faith, there's no reason to delay baptism. However, this approach makes no sense if baptism is the entrance to salvation and incorporation into the people of God. In this case, it's very important that adults be instructed in the Christian faith and life before baptism. The early church recognized this point and insisted on a period of catechesis for adults before baptism.

But why, then, did the early church (see Acts 2:41; 8:36-38) baptize people immediately upon their expressing faith in Jesus? Because in the early decades of Christianity, the vast majority of converts were Jewish. They were already instructed in the fundamentals of biblical faith. They already knew how the people of God should live. Thus no extensive period of instruction was necessary. However, as observed in chapter 5, once the church moved into the Gentile world, the church could no longer assume that converts knew the biblical tradition. Gentile converts certainly did not know how God's people should live. For that reason, the church developed the practice of catechesis.

Today, we live in an increasingly post-Christian world, at least in many countries with a Christian heritage. The church today cannot assume that converts know what they should know and live as they should live. Our situation today is more like the early church's experience with Gentile converts than its experience with Jewish converts. As a result, we should follow the example of the early church and insist on substantial instruction in the Christian faith and life.

Born Again in Baptism?

For centuries, the church identified baptism as the moment when we are born again (regenerated). It did so because of New Testament passages such as John 3 (which links being born again with being born of "water and Spirit" [v. 5]) and Titus 3:5 (which speaks of the washing of rebirth and the renewal of the Spirit). These passages tell us that in baptism we receive God's Spirit and new spiritual life—we are born again. This view is sometimes referred to as *baptismal regeneration*.

However, in the last two centuries, many evangelical Christians have argued that we are born again in a moment of dramatic conversion. Such conversion may happen before or after baptism and, in fact, has no connection with baptism at all. For many evangelicals, baptism is important only because it testifies to our having been born again in a conversion experience.

Evangelical theology has several valid points. It's true that baptism is no guarantee of salvation and that it is not absolutely necessary for salvation. It's also important to honor the fact that an experience of evangelical conversion is, for many Christians, the entry into the Christian life. At the same time, we have to admit that evangelical theology really has overlooked the importance of passages such as John 3 and Titus 3:5. These passages pretty clearly link baptism with rebirth.

Evangelicals have two problems with the idea of baptismal regeneration. First, they notice that many baptized people do not live as Christians and fall away from the faith. They conclude that baptism has not effected any real change. Second, they argue that being born again is a conversion experience, whereas people may or may not have a conversion experience in baptism.

In response, we can observe that many people who have had a born-again experience fail to live as Christians and fall away from the faith. Neither baptism nor a conversion experience guarantees salvation. Additionally, it is important to note that the New Testament does not portray rebirth as an experience, as many evangelicals do. The New Testament depicts rebirth as an act of God in which we receive the Holy Spirit and new life and are incorporated into Christ's body, the church. But nothing in the Bible demands that rebirth be an identifiable experience. Sometimes God's grace acts upon us in very quiet ways.

It's best, then, for the church today to recover the power of John 3 and Titus 3:5 and to see in baptism God's act of restoring the spiritual life that sin has destroyed. Such a recovery does not diminish the importance of conversion experiences. It simply reminds us that God's grace comes to us sacramentally through common things such as water.

Rebaptism?

Many years ago, at a denominationally sponsored theology conference, a participant asked a church leader what should be done in Latin America about church members who were former Roman Catholics and who, believing their baptism in the Catholic Church to be invalid, wanted to be baptized again. The leader indicated that he would approve rebaptisms for these members. There are several significant issues raised by this leader's response. These issues are present every time Christians ask to be baptized again simply because they believe their first baptism was meaningless.

Rebaptism makes lots of sense if we think of baptism as an act of human testimony. Believers who change from being nominal Christians to living authentically as Christians may wish to offer public testimony to the change. Rebaptism may seem like a logical way of offering testimony. In this view, the importance of baptism lies in its ability to express what we think and feel and experience.

However, the church has always taught that rebaptism makes no sense if we think of it as an act of God that initiates us into salvation. Instead of being a way of expressing what we think and feel and experience, baptism is the event in which God comes to us and draws us into the people of God. It truly draws us into salvation. From this fact the church has always concluded that baptism is a one-time event. Even if we later fall away or grow cold in our spiritual life, the fact remains that in baptism God has come to us. We don't need a rebaptism to bring God to us again. In this sense, baptism is like a marriage ceremony. We don't have to get remarried to our spouse after an argument. Even if a marriage finds new vitality after a period of coldness, there is no need to be married all over again. We simply accept that we are married and seek to renew it. It's true that some people renew their marriage vows; however, such renewal is not a remarriage. In the same way, there is never any reason to be rebaptized (except in the case of baptisms not performed in the name of the Trinity—but those aren't valid baptisms to begin with). Perhaps the church should develop a ritual of reconsecration so that those who wish to renew their baptismal vows can do so without repeating baptism.

8

A SHORT MEDITATION ON BAPTISM

Baptism is a symbol, a likeness.

The water that flows over the body shows forth the grace that flows over the soul.

The water that washes worldly things, when consecrated, washes away sin.

The water in which we lie is the tomb that swallows us as we die with Jesus.

The water from which we emerge is the open grave releasing us into the new life of the resurrection.

Baptism is a medium. The water, the words of consecration, and the words of proclamation are media through which God's grace approaches us. In these simple, common realities God comes to us just as God came to us in the humble man from Nazareth. It is God's way to be hidden but also revealed to us in ordinary things like water and words.

Baptism is a mirror. Those without faith see water and hear words. Those with faith see God's action in the water; they hear God's proclamation in the words. Baptism is thus a reflection of something divine. With faith we see through the physical water and hear through the human words and see and hear God.

Baptism is a token. As needy beings, we need tokens to assure us of love. Baptism is God's token. By sharing in it and witnessing it, our confidence in God is strengthened, for it is the divine proclamation that we belong to God.

Baptism is a performance. Like music, grace must be performed to be actual. In baptism, God performs grace through the minister, the congregation, and the baptismal candidates. The performance of baptism makes grace real in the soul. That is why we should never minimize the ceremony of baptism. Instead, we should honor it as a ceremony of performance.

COMMUNION

9

THE HISTORY OF COMMUNION

Unlike baptism, the other sacrament affirmed by Protestants has more than one name. It is commonly referred to as Communion, the Lord's Supper, and the Eucharist. Describing this sacrament as *Communion* highlights that through it we have communion or fellowship with God and with each other. Calling it the *Lord's Supper* draws attention to its origins in the ministry of Jesus. *Eucharist* (based on the Greek word for thanksgiving) emphasizes that thanksgiving and blessing are included in the ancient ceremony surrounding this sacrament.

Though there are several historical and biblical precedents for its practice, the history of this sacrament begins with Jesus, who instituted Communion at his final meal with the disciples. Two points deserve attention.

First, meals were quite important in the ministry of Jesus as symbols of the kingdom of God. The tradition of likening the kingdom of God to a great banquet began with Isaiah (Isa. 25:6). So when Jesus ate with tax-gatherers and sinners and when he multiplied loaves and fishes for the multitude, he was anticipating the kingdom of God. In these acts of eating and feeding Jesus was declaring that the kingdom was present in a way that anticipated its complete arrival in the future. The final meal with the disciples was another opportunity to celebrate the presence of the kingdom. The sacrament of Communion, then, is closely connected to Jesus' preaching about the kingdom.

Second, the gospels of Matthew, Mark, and Luke all present the Last Supper as a Passover meal. As Jews, Jesus and the disciples gathered together during the festival of Passover to share in the ritual meal. The institution of the Last Supper was, so to speak, an appendix to the Passover meal. This reminds us that the sacrament of Communion has its roots in a Jewish celebration.

Our knowledge of the practice of Communion in the New Testament period comes mainly from 1 Cor. 10–11. In these chapters Paul criticized the Corinthians' practice of Communion at those points where he detected problems. There is much that these chapters don't tell us; however, they do tell us that Communion was a part of a community meal and that for Communion itself they used a single loaf of bread. We learn as well that Jesus' words at the Last Supper were well known, at least in Paul's churches.

Several Christian writers of the second century wrote about Communion, and we get a good picture of how it was practiced in the postapostolic church. We learn, for instance, that only those who had been baptized could participate in Communion. This is because only the baptized were considered to be members of the people of God. Even those in the process of catechesis were not allowed to participate in Communion—they had not yet been fully initiated into the Christian faith. Second-century writers tell us also that Communion took place each Sunday as a part of worship. It was accompanied by a confession of sins (in some form) and by a prayer of thanksgiving. A portion of the bread and wine were set aside and taken to those who were not able to partake of Communion during worship. These practices are still observed in the liturgy of many churches today.

What about the theology of Communion in the early church? For one thing, it was thought of as a sacrifice or offering of praise that the church offered to God. Communion was the offering that the church, as the priestly people of God, gave to God in the new covenant. It was also portrayed as the medicine of immortality—the spiritual food that nourished the soul and overcame the death that sin brought. Finally, early writers commonly saw the bread and wine as the body and blood of Jesus. Clearly they understood there was nothing magical about the bread and wine; in themselves they were simply bread and wine. But when they were consecrated by a prayer of blessing, they became (in some way) the flesh and blood of Jesus. By consuming the consecrated elements, Christians came to share in Christ's resurrected life and thus overcame death. The prayer of consecration came to be called the epiclesis (Greek for "calling down or upon"), since in this prayer the congregation asked the Holy Spirit to come upon the bread and cup and make those elements become for them the body and blood of Christ.

The next major development in the theology of Communion came many centuries later, in the Middle Ages. In the Western, Latin-speaking churches, questions were raised about the precise sense in which the bread and wine were Christ's body and blood. After much dialogue, the Western church began to think of the bread and wine as *becoming* the body and blood. The term used to describe this belief was "transubstantiation." This was the idea that when consecrated, the bread and wine retained only the appearance of bread and wine. In truth, they were no longer bread and wine but were truly the body and blood of Christ. Consecration thus produced a miraculous transformation of the elements. Transubstantiation remains the teaching of the Roman Catholic Church today.

Alongside the idea of transubstantiation, the Western churches of the Middle Ages developed the belief that in Communion Jesus Christ's sacrifice was repeated. If, they reasoned, Jesus' body and blood were truly present in Communion, then Christ's body was once again broken and his blood was once again spilled, just as on the cross. Communion, then, was for them a reenactment of the crucifixion.

With the rise of the Protestant Reformation, the theology of Communion was subject to rethinking. Protestants found the idea of transubstantiation to be overly complicated and not supported by the New Testament. They also found no biblical support for the idea that Christ's crucifixion was reenacted in Communion.

However, this agreement about what Communion was *not* didn't produce agreement about what Communion *was*. Martin Luther felt that Jesus' words ("this is my body . . . this is my blood" [see Matt. 26:26-28]) should be taken literally. He believed that in a mysterious way the resurrected, glorified Jesus was present in the bread and wine. Luther rejected transubstantiation, believing that the bread and wine continued to be bread and wine; however, Jesus was, in Luther's words, "in, with, and under" the bread and wine. So those who shared in Communion were feeding on the resurrected body and blood of Jesus.

The Anabaptists, however, felt that Luther's view took Jesus' words too literally. They did not believe that Jesus was really present in the Communion elements. For them, the most important part of Jesus' words was the command, "Do this in remembrance of me" (Luke 22:19). Communion thus became for them an act of remembrance. The purpose of Communion, they held, was to recollect and declare Jesus' death.

John Calvin felt that both Luther and the Anabaptists had it wrong. He agreed with Luther and the Catholic tradition that Communion was (in some sense) about feeding on Christ and thus nourishing the souls of believers; he did not believe that remembrance was the most important thing about Communion. However, he believed that Luther and the Catholics took Jesus' words ("this is my body") too literally. Calvin wanted an alternative to the Anabaptists (on the one hand) and Luther and the Catholics (on the other hand). His alternative was to believe that in Communion the faithful truly did feed on Christ; however, they fed on him in a spiritual way. In Communion, the Holy Spirit brought believers into spiritual communion with the resurrected Christ. They took Christ's resurrected life into theirs, but spiritually, not physically. As a result, Calvin did not believe that Christ was present in the Communion elements. Still, it was in eating these elements that believers fed spiritually on Christ and were spiritually nourished.

There has been no important development in the theology of Communion since the Reformation. Lutherans still believe that Christ's body and blood are truly present in the bread and wine. Anabaptists still put the emphasis on remembrance. Calvinists (such as the Presbyterian Church) still think in terms of spiritual feeding. Evangelicals in America tend to side with the Anabaptists on this issue.

What about the Wesleyan churches? As with baptism, we find several views. John Wesley's views were shaped by his own Church of England, whose theology of Communion was rooted in the tradition of John Calvin. Thus Free Methodists take the approach that the resurrected Christ is truly present in the act of Communion; however, in the eating and drinking we receive Christ's body in a spiritual manner, not in a physical manner.[14] This is the traditional Calvinist language of the Church of England. The Church of the Nazarene, however, takes an Anabaptist approach: "The Memorial and Communion Supper . . . is essentially a New Testament sacrament, declarative of His sacrificial death. . . . By it [believers] show forth the Lord's death till He come again."[15] The statements of other churches with a Wesleyan background, such as the Wesleyan Church and the Church of God (Anderson), don't specify a particular understanding of Communion.

10
THE THEOLOGY OF COMMUNION

As the short historical review of the last chapter showed us, Communion is a rich reality, one with many sides. No single theme can really exhaust the meaning of Communion. Let's look at what the New Testament has to say.

Thanksgiving and Blessing

"He took a cup, and after giving thanks . . ." (Matt. 26:27); "The cup of blessing that we bless . . ." (1 Cor. 10:16). One of the most prominent aspects of Communion is the giving of thanks to God. The fact that Jesus offered thanks reminds us of his Jewish heritage, in which prayers of blessing and thanksgiving abound. Jesus' offering of thanks passed over into the liturgy of the early church, which included prayers of thanksgiving and blessing in its ritual for Communion.

The Blood of the New Covenant

As the Gospels present it, Jesus saw the wine of the Last Supper as blood that effected a new covenant (Matt. 26:28). Exodus relates that Moses inaugurated the first covenant by spilling the blood of oxen (24:3-

8). Jesus saw that his own death—his blood—would inaugurate a new covenant. To celebrate Communion, then, is to participate in the new covenant and to honor the blood that effected it.

The Kingdom of God

As we've seen, meals in the ministry of Jesus signified the coming kingdom of God. They were ways of living the future kingdom in the present. So it is not surprising that Jesus used his final meal to declare, "I confer on you . . . a kingdom, so that you may eat and drink at my table in my kingdom" (Luke 22:29-30). The Last Supper was, for Jesus, an anticipation of the fullness of God's kingdom, which would be like a great banquet, at which many "will come from east and west, from north and south, and will eat in the kingdom of God" (13:29). To share in Communion today is likewise to anticipate that kingdom, with its banquet. It is to dwell now in the power of the coming kingdom.

Communion

The idea of Communion is taken from Paul's words in 1 Corinthians: "The cup of blessing that we bless, is it not a sharing in the blood of Christ? The bread that we break, is it not a sharing in the body of Christ?" (10:16). To eat the bread and drink from the cup is to share in Christ's body and blood. In this act of eating and drinking we are united with the risen Lord. It was because of this aspect of the Lord's Supper that many early Christian writers connected the Supper with 2 Pet. 1:4, which speaks of becoming "participants in the divine nature." In the Supper, we share in Christ's glorified body and thus in his eternal life and divine nature.

Proclamation

As Paul noted, "As often as you eat this bread and drink the cup, you proclaim the Lord's death until he comes" (1 Cor. 11:26). This act of eating and drinking is thus an act of declaring. By sharing in Communion we preach—not with words but with sacred action, for our celebration of the Lord's Supper reenacts Jesus' own proclamation of his death. However, Communion should always be accompanied by the proclamation of the gospel in words. That is why many churches embed the celebration of Communion in a liturgy. A liturgy is an outline of worship that is used each Sunday. It includes scriptural readings that surround Communion. In this way, churches ensure that the gospel is proclaimed both by symbolic act and by words.

Remembrance

Jesus said, "Do this in remembrance of me" (Luke 22:19). However, our participation in the Lord's Supper is much more than an act of remembrance in the ordinary sense. Many acts of remembrance are acts of simple recollection. We remember telephone numbers and addresses, birth dates and names, and so on. Such acts of remembrance are really exercises in finding information. To speak of Communion as remembrance, however, is to say that we "re-call" that event—we call it from the past into the present. In Communion we find our place in the Last Supper. It is no longer a historical event in the past. Instead, through remembrance it becomes a present reality in which we participate. In liturgical churches, remembrance is formally celebrated in the anamnesis (Greek for "recalling" or "recollecting"), which is that part of the liturgy that specifically recalls Christ's death and resurrection.

Unity

In Communion we are united, not only with the risen Lord but also with each other. As Paul affirmed, "Because there is one bread, we who are many are one body, for we all partake of the one bread" (1 Cor. 10:17). Paul observed that the church, which is composed of many individuals, becomes one in the act of Communion. By sharing in the one bread, which is a sharing in Christ's body, we become the one body of Christ. Communion thus completes what baptism begins. In baptism we are initiated into Christ's body by being identified with him. In Communion we are fully incorporated into his body, the church.

In its preaching, teaching, and practice, every congregation should give attention to each of these aspects of Communion. Distortion results when we emphasize only one or two and neglect the others. Evangelical Christians have done well with emphasizing remembrance and proclamation; however, they have tended to ignore the other aspects. But respect for the Bible demands that we pay heed to the full range of truth contained in its teaching about the Lord's Supper.

11

DISAGREEMENTS ABOUT COMMUNION

As with baptism, Communion has engendered much discussion throughout history about its meaning and practice. Disagreements over these issues continue to distinguish present-day faith communities from each other. What follows are several of the most important areas of debate.

Open vs. Closed Communion

Some churches, notably the Roman Catholic Church and Orthodox churches, practice closed Communion. This means that in order to participate in Communion, a person must be a member of the church (i.e., denomination) in which Communion is being offered. The alternative is open Communion, in which denominational membership is not required.

The Roman Catholic Church practices closed Communion because it maintains that a degree of alienation exists between it and other Christian groups. Although it acknowledges that Protestants are Christian believers, it does not believe they are in full communion (i.e., unity) with the Catholic Church. So it holds that it would be inappropriate for Protestants to share in Communion offered by the Roman Catholic Church. Such sharing would imply more unity than actually exists. The Orthodox churches have the same view and do not share Communion with Protestants, Roman Catholics, or any other Christian group.

Most Protestant denominations practice open Communion. Some (for example, the Lutheran Church–Missouri Synod) do not. Churches in the Wesleyan tradition do practice open Communion. This is because they do not insist on institutional unity as a requirement for Communion. All Christians, they believe, are in communion with the body of Christ, regardless of institutional affiliation.

Use of Wine vs. Grape Juice

Until the nineteenth century, congregations of all types used wine in Communion. In nineteenth-century America, however, widespread abuse of alcohol led to the prohibition movement, which aimed at eliminating the sale and use of alcohol. As a way of supporting the ideals of this movement, some churches adopted grape juice as a substitute for wine in Communion. Some still use wine.

This is one of those nonessential issues about which we should all adopt an attitude of generosity and tolerance. There is no good reason to think that the use of wine is necessary for valid Communion; grape juice is perfectly acceptable. At the same time, those who use grape juice should not criticize those who use wine or assume an attitude of moral superiority. The church has, over the centuries, wisely observed that God grants to the church wide latitude in worship practices. The choice between wine and grape juice is one of those practices where local circumstances and traditions can be allowed to determine the matter.

The Real Presence of Jesus in the Elements

As we observed earlier, churches have disagreed about whether the body and blood of the risen Lord are truly present in the act of Communion. The Roman Catholic Church, the Orthodox churches, and the Lutheran churches assert that Christ's body and blood are truly present. Many Protestant groups deny this presence. Churches in the Calvinist tradition affirm a kind of spiritual presence.

Many Protestants feel negatively toward the idea of the real presence because they disagree with the Catholic idea of transubstantiation. However, it's possible to believe (with Lutheran and Orthodox Christians) in the real presence without affirming the idea of transubstantiation. At any rate, the issue for Protestants will be the Bible's teaching. Does Scripture assert the real presence?

Debates in the past have, unfortunately, focused on the question of whether the words "this is my body . . . this is my blood" are to be understood literally or as a metaphor. This is a difficult question to answer. The difficulty is greater if we focus on questions about whether the bread becomes Christ's body and whether Christ is physically present in the elements. Everything becomes simpler if we listen to Paul's words, "The cup of blessing that we bless, is it not a sharing in the blood of Christ? The bread that we break, is it not a sharing in the body of Christ?" (1 Cor. 10:16). These words tells us that the act of eating and drinking is truly an act by which we come to share in the glorified Jesus Christ and are united with him in the unity of his divinity and humanity. In Communion, as in no other event, we participate in Christ's body, which is both the church on earth and also his glorified, heavenly body.

The idea of Christ's real presence, then, as affirmed by Orthodox, Catholic, and Lutheran Christians, rests on an authentic scriptural basis. Even churches that do not teach the real presence precisely as these churches do can still affirm (as does the Free Methodist Church) a vital connection between the Eucharistic elements and our sharing in Christ's body.

The Frequency of Communion

Ideas about how often Communion should be celebrated correspond to ideas about the real presence. Churches that teach the real presence of Christ in the bread and cup offer Communion weekly. Churches that emphasize Communion as remembrance and proclamation offer it less frequently, sometimes much less frequently.

The reason for the correspondence is simple. Christians who believe in the real presence believe that Communion is the most important way for us to achieve union with Jesus (com + munion means "union with"). They consequently feel it's important to receive Communion frequently. Christians who emphasize Communion as remembrance don't feel the need for frequent Communion. For them we should be remembering and proclaiming Christ's death all the time; Communion is simply a formal way of doing so as a congregation.

This last view sometimes leads to a casual attitude toward Communion. A variation of this way of thinking often finds expression when someone says, "If we celebrate Communion too often (more than three for four times a year), it will become routine and stale." This is an unusual idea. We would never think of saying, "If we eat pancakes (or ham or tomatoes or apples or whatever your favorite food is) more than three or four times a year, we'll get bored with the routine. Let's keep pancakes special by having them only once in a while." Many of us believe there is no such thing as having pancakes too often; likewise many Christians believe it is impossible to share in Communion too often.

So, how often should a congregation celebrate the Lord's Supper? There are two considerations, one scriptural and the other traditional. From Scripture, we find that Paul saw the Lord's Supper as a sharing in Christ (see 1 Cor. 10:16). Notice that Paul did not say that the Supper symbolizes our union with Christ. He said that the Supper *is* our sharing in Christ. This Supper is the event in which it happens. If so, then frequent Communion should be the rule. From tradition, we observe that Communion was celebrated weekly in the early church. It is significant that John Wesley regarded weekly Communion as a minimum; he counseled Christians to celebrate Communion as frequently as possible. The Christian tradition thus supports the practice of frequent Communion.

Who Can Share in Communion?

Even churches that practice open Communion still normally demand that those who share in Communion be baptized or at least have faith in Jesus as the Savior. However, it is worth noting that John Wesley saw the Lord's Supper as a "converting ordinance." Wesley believed that as the Spirit was leading people toward repentance and faith, participation in Communion could very well be a tool the Spirit uses. So Wesley would not restrict Communion to Christian disciples; it was available for everyone, even those earnestly seeking salvation.

Eating Unworthily

In 1 Cor. 11:26-29 Paul criticized the Corinthians for their Eucharistic practices. In Corinth Communion was a part of a community meal. Unfortunately, wealthy members brought plenty to eat while poorer members had little or nothing to eat. As a result, the Lord's Supper reflected the class divisions that existed in Roman society. Paul condemned the Corinthians for allowing the Supper to become a time of division instead of an opportunity for unity: "Whoever, therefore, eats the bread or drinks the cup of the Lord in an unworthy manner will be answerable for the body and blood of the Lord. Examine yourselves, and only then eat of the bread and drink of the cup" (vv. 27-28).

What did Paul mean by these words? Unfortunately, these words have often been taken to mean that no one who is unworthy should share in Communion. This misinterpretation has led to a lot of unhelpful soul-searching, with people trying to decide whether they are worthy or unworthy. This issue is easily settled: No one is worthy of sharing in Christ's body. No one is worthy of proclaiming his death. The most mature, godly Christian is as unworthy as the greatest sinner. Jesus invites us to share in his Supper as an act of grace; that is why everyone is welcome. So Paul's words are not about whether or not we are worthy of sharing in Communion. We are not.

So what was Paul saying? He was saying that we must take care not to eat in an unworthy manner, that is, in a way that contradicts what the Supper is about. The Supper makes us the one body of Christ. But eating in a way that causes division in the body (as the Corinthians did) negates the unity that is at the heart of Communion. To perform Communion in this way is to eat it unworthily.

12

A SHORT MEDITATION ON THE LORD'S SUPPER

The Lord's Supper is a symbol because it is a likeness. In this Supper physical food feeds the soul. Our souls need food just as our bodies need food. Our souls need Jesus, the bread from heaven, whose flesh is true food.

However, because we are bodily creatures, we receive the bread of heaven through the medium of the Eucharistic bread and cup. We are not creatures of pure spirit; the heavenly bread does not come to us in a purely spiritual way. Instead it comes to us in and through physical bread and the physical cup.

And just as with the water of baptism, in the Eucharistic elements faith sees, not simply the bread and the cup, but the body and blood of Jesus. As in a mirror, we see the physical elements but we also see through them to the heavenly reality. We drink from the cup and taste the blood of the covenant. We eat the bread and receive the bread of life.

The Lord's Supper is also a token. Like gifts given, the Eucharistic elements are simply physical things, in themselves insignificant. But by a miracle of grace and consecration, the insignificant becomes signifying, just as a gift, in itself an insignificant material thing, signifies the giver's love.

Finally, the Lord's Supper performs grace. It is an act. Human beings of flesh and blood engage in the act of eating and thereby recall, proclaim, and feed on Christ. We receive God's grace in the doing of the Lord's Supper. The ceremony, the words, and the ritual of the Supper are thus of great importance. They actualize grace in the soul.

13

OTHER SACRAMENTAL PRACTICES

Every church has practices it categorizes as sacraments (or ordinances); however, there are other practices that have a sacramental character. They are not sacraments but are sacrament-like. Like sacraments, they are physical things or events that mediate God's grace to us.

Preaching, for instance, has a sacramental quality. Like the elements of the sacraments, preaching is (from one perspective) simply something physical: words conveyed by sound, bodily gestures, and so on. But the physical activity of preaching can be a sacramental medium for God's grace and presence. These ordinary, human words can, with God's help, become the word of God for us, just as the Eucharistic bread and cup can become the body and blood of Christ for us. For this reason, every act of preaching should be accompanied by a prayer of consecration. We should pray that just as God consecrates water so that it can be a medium for grace, so God would consecrate the words of the preacher so that they can be a medium for grace.

The Bible also has a sacramental character. From one perspective, it is a simple material object—a relic from an ancient time and culture. But from the perspective of faith, the Bible has the power to bring God's grace and revelation to us. Like the sacraments, it is a physical thing that, with consecrated reading, becomes a medium of grace.

CONCLUSION

We could list many other practices that have a sacramental character, such as prayer, good works, confession, and forgiveness, but attempting such an exhaustive list is unnecessary. We should instead strive to cultivate a sacramental understanding of reality. With such an understanding we would see everything as a medium of divine grace. Everything around us would be a mirror, reflecting God's presence. Everything would be a symbol, providing a likeness of grace's work in the soul. Everything would be a token, a gift that assures us of God's love. And we would see everything as a performance of grace, each thing playing its role in the great drama of salvation.

NOTES

1. "The Baptist Faith and Message," Southern Baptist Convention, http://www.sbc.net/bfm/bfm2000.asp#vii (accessed May 28, 2010).

2. "An Introduction to Baptism," Flood Church, http://www.diveintoflood.com/media/104_Baptism.pdf (accessed May 28, 2010).

3. "Our 16 Fundamental Truths," General Council of the Assemblies of God, http://ag.org/top/Beliefs/Statement_of_Fundamental_Truths/sft_full.cfm#6 (accessed May 28, 2010).

4. "Our Beliefs—Sacraments," The Salvation Army, http://www.salvationarmy.org/ind%5Cwww_ind.nsf/vw-sublinks/80256E520050A2E280256C140045D031?openDocument.

5. "What About . . . Communion?" Calvary Chapel Cheyenne, http://www.calvarychapelcheyenne.org/01%20Church/communion.html (accessed May 28, 2010).

6. "The Baptist Faith and Message," Southern Baptist Convention.

7. Ibid.

8. Augustine, *On the Catechising of the Uninstructed*, 26.50.

9. As, for example, at the Assemblies of God Web site, http://enrichmentjournal.ag.org/200002/078_urgency_baptism.cfm; the Christian Research Institute site, http://www.equip.org/perspectives/christian-baptism; and many other places on the Internet.

10. The Donatist controversy was a complex affair and affected the churches of North Africa (modern-day Tunisia and Libya). It began in the early 300s and continued for more than a century. There were many issues at stake; the focus here is on the sacramental issues.

11. *Manual/2009–2013: Church of the Nazarene* (Kansas City: Nazarene Publishing House, 2009), par. 803.

12. Other passages that understand baptism as a washing are Eph. 5:25-26; 1 Cor. 6:11; and Titus 3:5.

13. *Manual/2009–2013*, par. 800.3.

14. "Articles of Religion—The Church," Free Methodist Church, http://www.freemethodistchurch.org/Sections/About%20Us/Beliefs/Doctrines/Articles%2014-16.htm (accessed November 5, 2010).

15. "Preamble and Articles of Faith," Church of the Nazarene, http://www.nazarene.org/ministries/administration/visitorcenter/articles/display.aspx (accessed November 5, 2010). The Church of the Nazarene's theology of Communion differs from that of other Wesleyan churches because the Church of the Nazarene arose as a result of mergers. The merging groups that formed the Church of the Nazarene brought different theologies to the merger.

GLOSSARY

Anabaptism: A religious movement that began in the 1520s. It emphasized nonviolence, rejected infant baptism, and regarded Communion strictly as a remembrance and proclamation. It is represented today by the Amish, Mennonites, and Hutterites.

Anamnesis: The Greek word for "remembrance" or "recollection." It is the part of the liturgy in which the congregation recites affirmations of Christ's death, resurrection, and ascension to heaven.

Anglican Church: Another term for the Church of England. John Wesley was a priest in the Church of England.

Anointing of the sick: One of the sacraments of the Roman Catholic Church. In this sacrament a priest anoints a sick person with oil. As a sacrament it imparts grace to the soul of the sick person. It is sometimes referred to as the "last rites."

Baptismal regeneration: The idea that spiritual rebirth (regeneration) happens in baptism.

Baptism with the Holy Spirit: The event described in Acts 2 and elsewhere in which believers receive the Holy Spirit. For many churches this event coincides with water baptism; for others it is a distinct event after baptism.

Catechesis: Refers to instruction in the Christian faith prior to baptism (for adult converts) or to confirmation (for those baptized as infants).

Chrismation: A sacrament in the Orthodox churches. It is an anointing with oil, is performed with baptism, and signifies receiving the Holy Spirit.

Confirmation: The ceremony in which someone who has been baptized publicly affirms the Christian faith. In the Roman Catholic Church it is a sacrament. In other churches it is a nonsacramental practice.

Consecration: The act of devoting something to God and God's use. In the practice of the sacraments, it refers to praying that the water of baptism and the bread and cup of Communion become means of grace.

Consubstantiation: A term sometimes used to describe the Lutheran view that in Communion Christ's body and blood come to be in, with, and under the bread and cup.

Donatism: A movement that began in the early 300s in North Africa. One of the issues in this controversy concerned the question of whether a priest who is morally or spiritually imperfect can perform the sacraments validly.

Epiclesis: The part of the liturgy in which the Holy Spirit is invited to come upon the bread and cup of Communion and thus consecrate them.

Eucharist: One of the terms for Communion. It is based on the Greek word for thanksgiving.

Gnosticism: A second-century movement that held that the material world is evil.

Grace: God's kindness toward us and presence among us.

Liturgy: A word derived from a Greek word meaning "the work of the people" or "public service." It came to mean "the work of the people" in worship. It generally refers to the order of worship in churches that use the same outline and prayers each week.

Matrimony: Marriage, one of the sacraments of the Roman Catholic Church.

Memorial: One of the aspects of Communion, according to which Communion is the act of remembering Christ's death.

Ordinance: A term that some churches use instead of sacrament. It signifies those practices of the church that Jesus directly ordained.

Ordination: The act of consecrating someone for the church's ministry. Ordination is a sacrament in the Roman Catholic Church. Most churches stipulate that only ordained ministers can perform sacraments.

Pietism: A Protestant movement of the 1600s and 1700s. It sought to revive spiritual life in Protestant churches. It emphasized practice more than belief. John Wesley was heavily influenced by Pietism.

Reconciliation: One of the sacraments of the Roman Catholic Church. It is also known as penance. It involves repentance and confession of sins.

Regeneration: Another word for spiritual rebirth or being born again.

Revivalism: A movement arising from the Great Awakenings of the 1700s and early 1800s. It sought to find a way of creating and sustaining revivals.

Sacrament: Traditionally understood as a visible sign of grace.

Transubstantiation: Refers to the Roman Catholic teaching that the bread and wine of Communion become the body and blood of Christ.

BIBLIOGRAPHY

"Baptism, Eucharist and Ministry." Faith and Order Paper No. 111. Geneva: World Council of Churches, 1982. http://www.oikoumene.org/fileadmin/files/wcc-main/documents/p2/FO1982_111_en.pdf.

Borgen, Ole E. *John Wesley on the Sacraments: A Theological Study*. Grand Rapids: Zondervan, 1986.

Powell, Samuel M. *Discovering Our Christian Faith*. Kansas City: Beacon Hill Press of Kansas City, 2008.

______. *A Theology of Christian Spirituality*. Nashville: Abingdon Press, 2005.

Staples, Rob L. *Outward Sign and Inward Grace: The Place of Sacraments in Wesleyan Spirituality*. Kansas City: Beacon Hill Press of Kansas City, 1991.